ALEX
KUSKOWSKI

A FUN AND CREATIVE INTRODUCTION TO FIBER ART

COOL

KNITTING

for KIDS

**Checkerboard
Library**

An Imprint of Abdo Publishing
www.abdopublishing.com

VISIT US AT WWW.ABDOPUBLISHING.COM

Published by Abdo Publishing, a division of ABDO, PO Box 398166, Minneapolis, Minnesota 55439. Copyright © 2015 by Abdo Consulting Group, Inc. International copyrights reserved in all countries. No part of this book may be reproduced in any form without written permission from the publisher. Checkerboard Library™ is a trademark and logo of Abdo Publishing.

Printed in the United States of America, North Mankato, Minnesota
062014
092014

THIS BOOK CONTAINS
RECYCLED MATERIALS

Design and Production: Anders Hanson, Mighty Media, Inc.
Series Editor: Liz Salzmann
Photo Credits: Anders Hanson, Shutterstock

The following manufacturers/names appearing in this book are trademarks: Boye®, Kool-Aid®

Library of Congress Cataloging-in-Publication Data
Kuskowski, Alex., author.
  Cool knitting for kids : a fun and creative introduction to fiber art / Alex Kuskowski.
     pages cm. -- (Cool fiber art)
  Audience: Ages 8-10.
  Includes bibliographical references and index.
  ISBN 978-1-62403-308-7 (alk. paper)
  1. Knitting--Juvenile literature. I. Title.
  TT820.K874 2015
  746.43'2--dc23
                            2013043077

To Adult Helpers

This is your chance to assist someone new to crafting! As children learn to craft they develop new skills, gain confidence, and make cool things. These activities are designed to help children learn how to make their own craft projects. Some activities may need more assistance than others. Be there to offer guidance when they need it. Encourage them to do as much as they can on their own. Be a cheerleader for their creativity.

Before getting started remember to lay down ground rules for using the crafting tools and cleaning up. There should always be adult supervision when a child uses a sharp tool.

TABLE OF CONTENTS

Get into Knit

Discover the world of knitting! Knitting is the art of looping yarn to make fabric. You can knit something **funky** and cool. You can make almost anything.

Knitting is a great way to pass the time. All you need to start is needles and yarn. You can knit almost anywhere. Toss yarn and needles in a bag, and you're good to go!

You'll find a lot of ideas here to help you start knitting. Step-by-step instructions make learning a breeze. You'll love to show off the things you make. Just turn the page and get into knit!

Tools of the Trade

KNITTING NEEDLES

Knitting needles come in different sizes and shapes. The easiest needles to use are straight. A straight needle has a knob on one end and a point on the other.

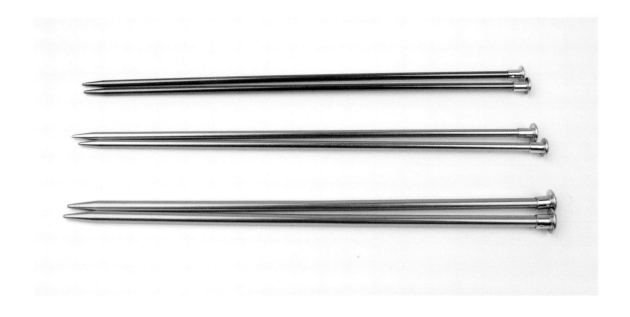

Needle Sizes

It's important to use the right size needles. Many **patterns** offer suggestions on what size needles to use. Skinny needles have low numbers such as 1, 2, and 3. Thick needles have high numbers such as 16, 17, and 18.

Yarn

You can't knit without yarn! Yarn comes in many sizes, weights, and shapes.

NATURAL FIBER

SYNTHETIC FIBER

Yarn Fiber

Yarn can be made with natural fibers or synthetic fibers. Natural fibers come from animals and plants, such as sheep and cotton. Synthetic fibers are man-made, such as acrylic and nylon.

YARN SHAPE

Yarn can have a traditional shape or a **novelty** shape. Traditional yarns are smooth and often have strands twisted together. Novelty yarns can be any shape from fur to ribbons.

YARN WEIGHT

Yarn weight ranges from super fine to super bulky. Thinner yarn uses smaller needles. See the chart for suggestions.

MEDIUM WEIGHT

BULKY WEIGHT

WEIGHT	SYMBOL	NEEDLE SIZE (MM)
SUPER FINE	1	1–3
FINE	2	3–5
LIGHT	3	5–7
MEDIUM	4	7–9
BULKY	5	9–11
SUPER BULKY	6	11 AND OVER

It's In the Bag

Keep a bag to hold your yarn, knitting needles, and general craft supplies like the ones below!

BAG

BEADS AND BUTTONS

MEASURING TAPE

PEN AND PAPER

SAFETY PINS

YARN

SCISSORS

THREAD

NEEDLES

GLUE

KNITTING NEEDLES

❖ Getting Started ❖

Knitting projects often use a **pattern**. The pattern says what you need for the project. It lists the yarn type, needle size, and more.

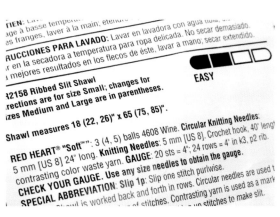

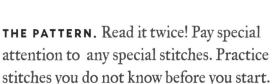

THE PATTERN. Read it twice! Pay special attention to any special stitches. Practice stitches you do not know before you start.

THE YARN. Many yarns come with a label. It can have a lot of important information.

READING A YARN LABEL

QUANTITY - The amount of yarn in the package.

FIBER CONTENT - What the yarn is made of.

DYE LOT - When yarn is dyed, it has a dye lot number. The exact color can vary from dye lot to dye lot. For a big project, use yarn from the same dye lot.

CARE INSTRUCTIONS - Shows how to wash the yarn.

RECOMMENDED NEEDLE SIZE - A suggestion of what size needles to use.

PATTERN ABBREVIATIONS

Patterns use **abbreviations**. They are easy to read once you know the basics!

Check the chart below for words you might not know.

ABBREVIATION	TERM
APPROX	APPROXIMATELY
BEG	BEGINNING
BLO	BACK LOOP ONLY
CH(S)	CHAIN(S)
CO	CAST ON
CONT	CONTINUE
DEC	DECREASE
INC	INCREASE
K	KNIT
PAT	PATTERN
PM	PLACE MARKER
ST(S)	STITCH(ES)
YO	YARN OVER

Basics

HOLDING THE NEEDLES

Hold the needles loosely between your thumbs and first fingers. Let your other fingers rest around the needles. The points should always face toward each other.

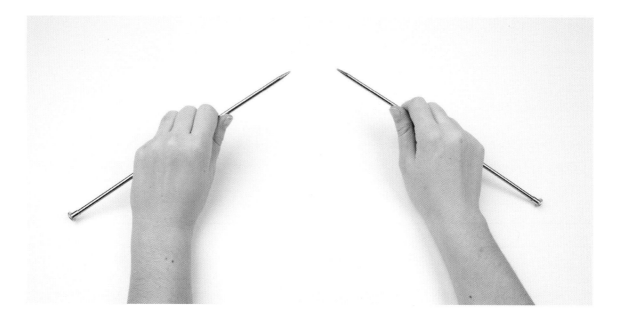

Counting Stitches

While knitting, check that you're making the correct number of stitches. It's important to count stitches. It can be easy to get off track.

To count stitches vertically, count the number of rows from top to bottom.

To count stitches horizontally, look at the top edge of the fabric. Count the number of knots from left to right.

TIP

Make a **gauge swatch** first. A gauge swatch is a 4-inch (10 cm) practice square. It is made using the same stitches as the **pattern**. The pattern says how many stitches fit inside the square. This helps you see if your stitches are the right size for the rest of the pattern.

STARTING UP

GET GOING WITH THESE DIRECTIONS!

WHAT YOU NEED

KNITTING NEEDLES (#6),
MEDIUM WEIGHT YARN

START WITH A SLIPKNOT

 Let the yarn tail hang in front of your left palm. Wrap the yarn loosely around your first two fingers.

 Pull the yarn forward between your second and third fingers. Push it up through the yarn over your fingers so it makes a loop.

 Hold both ends of the yarn in your left hand. Hold the loop in your right hand. Pull it snug.

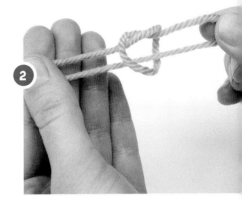

CASTING ON

 Make a slipknot. Stick a knitting needle through the loop. Pull on the ends to tighten the loop.

 Hold the needle in your right hand. Grab the yarn with your left hand. Twist it to the left to make a loop.

 Stick the needle through the loop. Pull the yarn tight. That is casting on one stitch. The instructions will say how many stitches to cast on for a project.

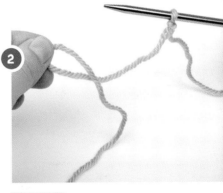

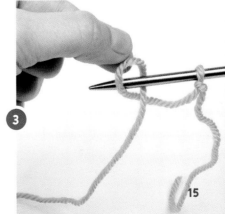

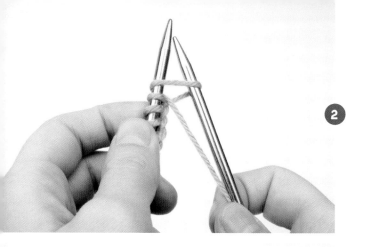

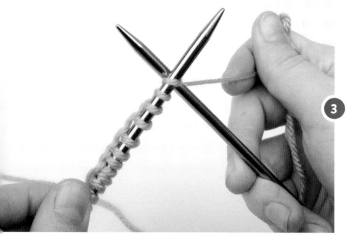

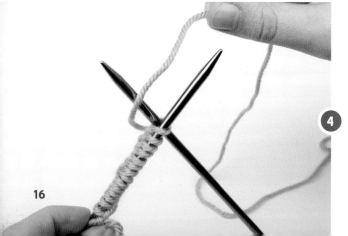

THE KNIT STITCH

1. Make a slipknot. Put it on a needle. Cast on 15 stitches.

2. Hold the needle with the stitches in your left hand. Stick the right-hand needle from left to right through the end stitch. The point of the right-hand needle should go toward the point of the left-hand needle.

3. When the right-hand needle is through the stitch, bring it behind the left-hand needle. Make an "x" with the needles. Keep the loose yarn behind both needles.

4. Wrap the loose yarn from left to right between the needles. This is called a yarn over.

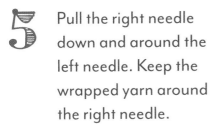 Pull the right needle down and around the left needle. Keep the wrapped yarn around the right needle.

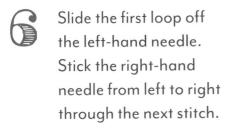 Slide the first loop off the left-hand needle. Stick the right-hand needle from left to right through the next stitch.

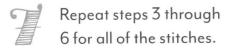 Repeat steps 3 through 6 for all of the stitches.

When you finish a row, the stitches will be on the right-hand needle. Switch the needle with the stitches to your left hand. Begin a new row of stitches.

BINDING OFF

 Knit stitch the first two stitches of a new row.

 Put the left needle through the rightmost stitch on the right needle.

Lift that stitch back over the other stitch and off the needle. Then drop the stitch from the left needle. Leave the other stitch on the right needle.

Knit the next stitch. Pull the rightmost stitch back over the other stitch and off the right needle. Let it go. Continue knitting and pulling stitches off one at a time. Stop when you get to the last loop.

Cut the yarn leaving a 7-inch (18 cm) tail. Remove the needle. Stick the tail through the last loop. Pull to tighten.

Thread the tail onto a yarn needle. Weave it through the knitting to hide the tail.

THE WHIPSTITCH

1 Cut a piece of yarn 12 inches (30.5 cm) long. Tie a knot at one end. Thread the other end onto a yarn needle.

2 Lay two pieces of knitting on top of each other. Line up the edges. Match the stitches up.

3 Push the needle up through both layers near the edge.

4 Bring the needle back underneath. Push it up ¼ inch (.5 cm) away from where you came up before. Pull it tight. This is called a whipstitch.

5 Move over another ¼ inch (.5 cm) and repeat the stitch. Keep going until the edges are sewn together. Tie a knot at the end. Weave the loose ends through the knitting.

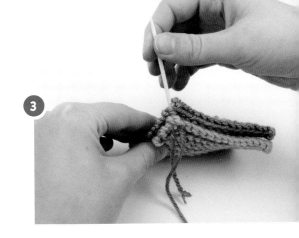

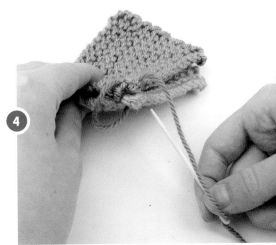

DYE IT,
YOU'LL LOVE IT!

COLOR YARN
WITH KOOL-AID!

WHAT YOU NEED

1 OUNCE 100% WOOL YARN
(WHITE), 4 6-INCH (15 CM)
PIECES OF COLORED
YARN, MEASURING TAPE,
SCISSORS, MICROWAVE-
SAFE BOWL, BAKING
SHEET, PLASTIC WRAP,
3 DRINKING GLASSES,
MEASURING CUP,
3 PACKETS UNSWEETENED
KOOL-AID (DIFFERENT
COLORS), SPOON, PLASTIC
GLOVES, SPRAY BOTTLE

1 Wind the yarn into a loop 8 inches (20 cm) long. Tie the pieces of colored yarn around the loop. Space them evenly around the loop.

2 Fill the bowl with hot water. Soak the yarn for 30 minutes. Cover the baking sheet with plastic wrap. Wring the water out of the yarn. Lay the yarn on the baking sheet.

3 Put 1 cup water in each drinking glass. Add a **packet** of Kool-Aid to each glass. Stir each glass.

4 Put on the gloves. Pour one of the glasses into the spray bottle. Spray it onto the yarn. Rinse the bottle. Pour another glass of Kool-Aid into the bottle. Spray it onto the yarn. Do the same with the third glass of Kool-Aid.

5 Wrap the plastic wrap around the yarn. Put it in the bowl. Microwave for 2 minutes. Let it cool for 2 minutes. Continue microwaving 2 minutes at a time until any leftover liquid is clear. Let it cool.

6 Unwrap the yarn and rinse it with water. Let the yarn dry for 6 hours.

PEEK-A-BOO MITTS

KEEP YOUR
WRISTS WARM!

WHAT YOU NEED

MEASURING TAPE, PENCIL,
PAPER, YARN (#5),
#10 KNITTING NEEDLES,
SCISSORS, YARN NEEDLE

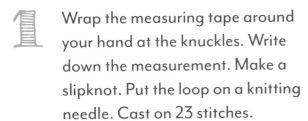

1. Wrap the measuring tape around your hand at the knuckles. Write down the measurement. Make a slipknot. Put the loop on a knitting needle. Cast on 23 stitches.

2. Knit stitch rows until the length matches your hand measurement. Bind off.

3. Thread the yarn needle with yarn. Fold the knitting in half. Line up the edge you bound off with the opposite edge. Starting at one corner, whipstitch them together for 1½ inches (4 cm).

4. Knot the yarn and cut it. Start sewing again 1½ inches (4 cm) away from where you stopped. Whipstitch to the corner. Knot the yarn and cut it. Weave any tails into the knitting. Turn the knitting inside out.

5. Repeat steps 1 through 4 to make a matching mitt.

COLORFUL COMBO SCARF

KNIT THIS
EASY SCARF!

WHAT YOU NEED

2 COLORS OF WORSTED
YARN (#4), #7 KNITTING
NEEDLES, MEASURING TAPE,
SCISSORS, YARN NEEDLE

1. Choose a color to start with. Make a slipknot. Put the loop on a knitting needle. Cast on 24 stitches.

2. Knit stitch rows until the knitting is 5 inches (13 cm) long. At the end of a row, cut the yarn. Leave a tail.

3. Tie the second color of yarn to the tail of the first color. Make the knot close to the knitting. Yarn over with the new color. Leave the tails alone.

4. Knit rows with the new color for 5 inches (13 cm). Switch back to the first color. Follow the same steps for changing yarn.

5. Keep knitting. Switch colors every 5 inches (13 cm). When the knitting is 60 inches (152 cm) long, bind off.

6. Use the yarn needle to weave in all the tails.

NEVER FELT BETTER

KNIT A BAG AND
FELT IT!

WHAT YOU NEED

4 OUNCES MULTICOLORED
WOOL YARN (#4),
#6 KNITTING NEEDLES,
MEASURING TAPE,
SCISSORS, YARN NEEDLE,
2 BOWLS, PLASTIC
GLOVES, LIQUID SOAP,
SPOON, TOWEL

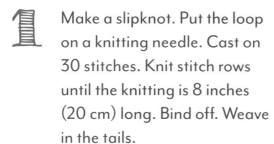

1. Make a slipknot. Put the loop on a knitting needle. Cast on 30 stitches. Knit stitch rows until the knitting is 8 inches (20 cm) long. Bind off. Weave in the tails.

2. Repeat step 1 to knit a second rectangle the same size.

3. Thread the yarn needle. Lay the two rectangles on top of each other. Line up the edges. Whipstitch the long sides together. Tie a knot and cut the yarn.

4. Whipstitch one of the short sides together to make a bag. Tie a knot and cut the yarn. Weave in the tails.

TIP

Use the yarn you dyed in the "Dye It, You'll Love It!" project (pages 20 and 21).

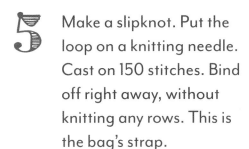

5 Make a slipknot. Put the loop on a knitting needle. Cast on 150 stitches. Bind off right away, without knitting any rows. This is the bag's strap.

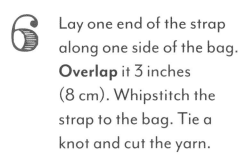

6 Lay one end of the strap along one side of the bag. **Overlap** it 3 inches (8 cm). Whipstitch the strap to the bag. Tie a knot and cut the yarn.

7 Whipstitch the other end of the strap to the other side of the bag.

8 Fill a bowl with hot water. Fill another bowl with ice water. Put on the gloves.

9 Put the bag and a spoonful of soap in the hot water. Twist, **scrub**, pull, and squeeze the bag for 5 minutes.

10 Put the bag in the ice water. Stir with your hands for 1 minute.

11 Put the bag back in the hot water. Keep switching between the bowls for 10 minutes.

12 Rinse the bag in the ice water. Squeeze out any extra water.

13 Lay the bag flat on a towel. Let it dry for 4 hours. Turn it over to dry the other side.

FELTING IS FUN!

Washing knitting in hot and cold water causes it to felt. The wool yarn becomes interlocked. The knitting shrinks and the stitches disappear. The knit project begins to look like felt fabric.

Keep Knitting!

You can knit almost anything! You can make cool stuff for yourself. Or make gifts for family and friends. There are tons of things to knit.

Explore craft and yarn stores. Check out books on knitting at the library. Look up knitting tips and projects online. Get inspired and create your own designs. Try making a hat, a handbag, or even a blanket. Or knit a piece of art. It's all about using your creativity!

GLOSSARY

ABBREVIATION – a short way to write a word.

FUNKY – cool or stylish in an unusual way.

GAUGE – to measure or judge.

NOVELTY – unusual or different.

OVERLAP – to make something lie partly on top of something else.

PACKET – a small and usually flat package.

PATTERN – a sample or guide used to make something.

SCRUB – to rub hard.

SWATCH – a sample piece of something such as a fabric.

WEB SITES

To learn more about fiber art, visit ABDO online at www.abdopublishing.com. Web sites about creative ways for kids to make fiber art are featured on our Book Links page. These links are routinely monitored and updated to provide the most current information available.

INDEX